D0382519

DRAWING ZENTANGLE® FANTASY WORLDS

Hannah Geddes

Gareth Stevens
PUBLISHING

Acknowledgments

The Zentangle® method was created by Rick Roberts and Maria Thomas.

"Zentangle"®, the Zentangle logo, "Anything is possible one stroke at a time", "Bijou", "Certified Zentangle Teacher"®, "CZT"®, "Zentangle Apprentice"®, and "Zentomology" are trademarks, service marks, or certification marks of Rick Roberts, Maria Thomas, and/or Zentangle Inc.

PERMISSION TO COPY ARTWORKS: The written instructions, designs, patterns, and projects in this book are intended for the personal use of the reader and may be reproduced for that purpose only. Any other use, especially commercial use, is forbidden under law without the written permission of the copyright holder.

All the tangles in this book are Zentangle® originals created by Rick Roberts and Maria Thomas, apart from: Daviso (page 17) by Katie Crommett CZT.

Please visit our website, www.garethstevens.com.
For a free color catalog of all our high-quality books,
call toll free 1-800-542-2595 or fax 1-877-542-2596.

CATALOGING-IN-PUBLICATION DATA

Names: Geddes, Hannah.
Title: Drawing Zentangle® fantasy worlds / Hannah Geddes.
Description: New York : Gareth Stevens Publishing, 2018. | Series: How to draw Zentangle® art | Includes index.
Identifiers: ISBN 9781538207239 (pbk.) | ISBN 9781538207178 (library bound) | ISBN 9781538207086 (6 pack)
Subjects: LCSH: Drawing--Technique--Juvenile literature. | Repetitive patterns (Decorative arts)--Juvenile literature. |
    Insects in art--Juvenile literature.
Classification: LCC NC730.G43 2018 | DDC 741.201'9--dc23

Published in 2018 by
Gareth Stevens Publishing
111 East 14th Street, Suite 349
New York, NY 10003

Step-outs and Zentangle® Inspired Artworks by Hannah Geddes
Text by Catherine Ard
Outline illustrations by Katy Jackson
Designed by Trudi Webb and Emma Randall
Edited by Frances Evans

Printed in China
CPSIA compliance information: Batch CS17GS: For further information contact
Gareth Stevens, New York, New York at 1-800-542-2595.

Contents

Imagine a World...

Zentangle® is a drawing method created by Rick Roberts and Maria Thomas. It teaches you how to create beautiful pieces of art using simple **patterns** called tangles. Tangling is a really fun, relaxing way to get creative, and it brings out the artist in everyone. You can tangle wherever and whenever the mood takes you!

It's time to create a fairy-tale kingdom! Bring your favorite **mythical** creatures to life with the magic of Zentangle®. You can find inspiration for your Zentangle® Inspired Artworks ("ZIAs") from fantasy books, movies, or your own imagination! We've chosen tangles that suit each fantastic creature. You can use the recommended tangles, or mix and match to create unique projects!

Pens and Pencils

Pencils are good for drawing "strings"(page 18) and for adding shade to your tangles. A 01 (0.25-mm) black pen is good for fine lines. Use a 05 (0.45-mm) or 08 (0.50-mm) pen to fill in bigger areas. You can use paints to brighten up your art, too!

Paper

Tangles are usually drawn on a square 3.5-inch (9 cm) tile made of thin cardboard. You can use any kind of paper, but if you want to make your tangles really special, use good quality art paper. Have some tracing paper on hand so you can trace the images in this book to use as outlines for your Zentangle® Inspired Artworks.

Useful Techniques

There are some special techniques you might come across when you tangle. A "highlight" is a gap or blank space in the lines of your tangles. Highlights can make your tangles look shiny!

An "aura" is a line traced around the inside or outside of a shape. Use auras to add a sense of movement to your art.

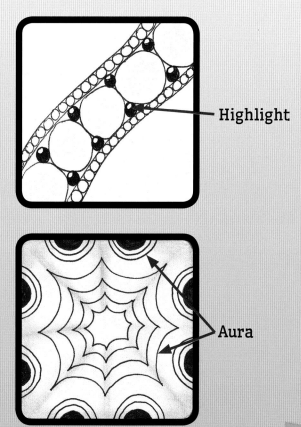

Highlight

Aura

Essential Tangles

Here are some fantastic tangles to get you started! You can practice drawing each tangle on a square tile (see step 1 on page 18 for instructions). Each project in this book has a tangle key that tells you where to find the instructions for the tangles that have been used.

Tipple

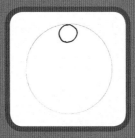

1. Start by drawing a small circle on your paper.

2. Add a few more circles around the first one. They can be any size you like.

3. Keep drawing circles of different sizes until the chosen space is full.

4. Shade in the spaces between the circles to finish your tangle.

Bales

1. Draw evenly-spaced **diagonal** lines across the paper.

2. Draw diagonal lines in the opposite direction to make a **grid**.

3. Draw bumps along the bottom of all of the lines you drew in step 1.

4. Then draw bumps along the top of these lines.

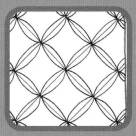

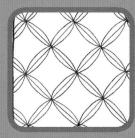

5. Repeat steps 3 and 4 on the diagonal lines that you drew in step 2.

6. Your pretty tangle is finished.

Keeko

1. Draw four **horizontal** lines next to each other. They should be the same length and equally spaced apart.

2. Draw another four lines next to the first set, but this time make the lines **vertical**.

3. Repeat steps 1 and 2 until the row is complete.

4. Underneath each set of four horizontal lines, draw a set of four vertical lines.

5. Draw a set of four horizontal lines underneath each set of vertical lines.

6. Fill the chosen area, and then add some shading to finish it.

Cadent

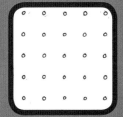 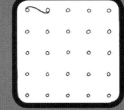 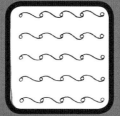 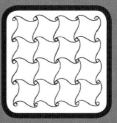 

1. Draw a grid made up of small circles.

2. Draw a curve from the top of the first circle to the bottom of the second circle.

3. Repeat this pattern across each horizontal row of circles.

4. Now, use the same pattern to join up the vertical lines of circles.

5. Your Cadent tangle is complete.

'Nzeppel

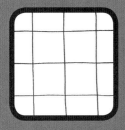 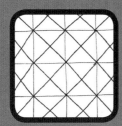 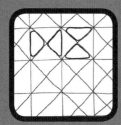  

1. Draw horizontal and vertical lines over the paper to make a grid.

2. Now draw diagonal lines in both directions over the paper. They should be evenly spaced so they run through the middle of each square in the grid.

3. Each square in the grid should now be split into four triangular sections. Draw around the shape of each triangle, but round off the corners to create this pebble-like effect.

4. Continue to fill each square with triangles, as shown.

5. Add some shading to finish your tangle.

Printemps

This tangle is perfect for creating swirly textures.

1. Draw a dot in the middle of your page. Then begin to draw a small **spiral** starting from the dot.

2. Continue drawing your spiral. You can make it as small or as big as you like.

3. Once the spiral is the size that you want, turn the line in to close up the shape. You should have a smooth circle around the edge.

4. Add more spiral shapes around the first one.

5. Continue drawing Printemps spirals until you have filled the space.

Vega

This crisscross tangle creates a lovely texture for the fur or scales on your magical creatures.

1. Draw two widely-spaced curved lines diagonally across the page.

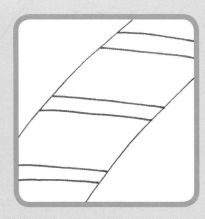

2. Now add pairs of diagonal lines between the curved lines.

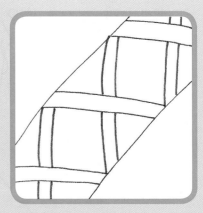

3. Add more pairs of diagonal lines going in the opposite direction. Stop drawing when you reach a line and continue on the other side.

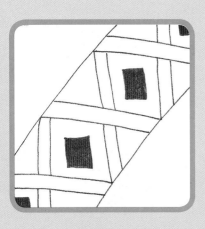

4. Draw a small diamond in the middle of each diamond-shaped space and fill it in with your pen.

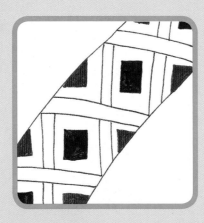

5. Now draw triangles in each of the triangular spaces and fill these in to finish the tangle.

6. Your tangle is complete! You can make the filled-in shapes bigger if you like.

Crescent Moon

With its dark dots and layers of rings, this tangle is perfect for a pair of beautiful wings.

1. Draw small semicircles around the edge of the area and fill them in.

2. Draw two arches, or auras, around each semicircle.

3. Leave a gap and draw joined-up arches that follow the shape of the auras, but do not reach the edge of the tangle area.

4. Repeat this pattern, getting smaller each time, until you reach the middle. These are also auras!

5. Draw pencil lines through the points of the joined-up arches and smudge for a **3-D** effect.

Tangle Tip!
Change the look of this tangle by using different shapes for the auras.

Jonqual

This dramatic 3-D tangle will bring your fantasy creatures to life.

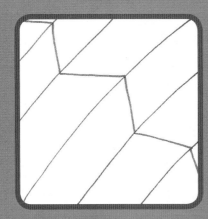

1. Draw evenly-spaced diagonal lines across the paper.

2. Draw a zigzag line in the opposite direction across the diagonals.

3. Add evenly-spaced zigzags following the shape of the first one. Starting in the second row, fill in every other rectangle with your pen.

4. Continue filling in every other rectangle in every other row until you have finished.

Tangle Tip!
Experiment with how you fill in the rectangles or the shape of the grid to change up this tangle.

Finery

Use this delicate tangle for a flowing effect on animals' manes and tails.

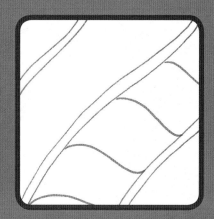

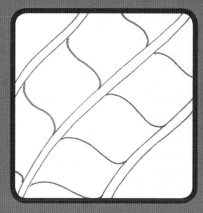

1. Draw three curvy diagonal bands across the paper.

2. Add evenly-spaced curved lines between the middle and right-hand bands. Each curved line looks like a stretched, sideways "S."

3. Now add curved lines between the middle and left-hand bands going in the opposite direction.

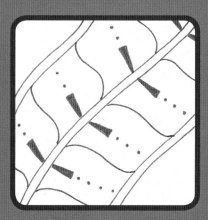

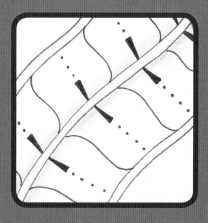

4. Draw narrow triangles between each pair of curved lines on either side of the middle band. Fill in the triangles and add some dots leading to the outer bands.

5. Shade and smudge on either side of the middle band to finish.

Tortuca

This grid of neat and tidy spirals is great for creating curly fur or a pretty floral pattern.

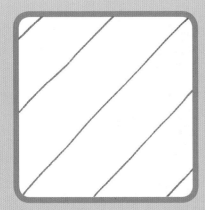

1. Draw evenly-spaced diagonal lines across the paper.

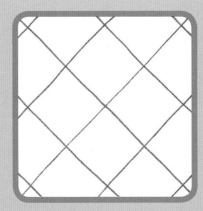

2. Add more diagonal lines in the opposite direction to form a grid of diamonds.

3. Draw a spiral inside a diamond, starting at the edge and working your way into the middle.

4. Fill every square with a spiral, always starting at the same place in each square.

5. Your pretty spiral tangle is ready!

Tangle Tip!

Change the look of Tortuca by adding shading, or by filling in the gaps between the spirals with your pen.

Huggins

Simply join the dots to reveal a totally bold basket weave tangle!

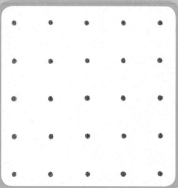

1. Begin by drawing a grid of small, evenly-spaced dots.

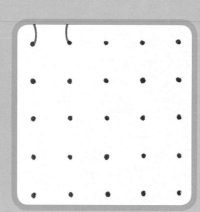

2. Starting in the top left corner, draw small curved lines from the top of the paper to the right side of the first dot and the left side of the second dot.

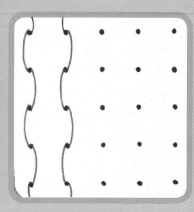

3. Draw curved lines to the dots below that go in the opposite direction from the ones above. Continue to add more curves down the paper, always alternating their direction.

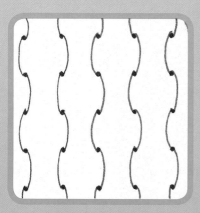

4. Repeat this pattern to fill every vertical row.

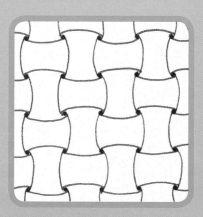

5. Now draw pairs of curves in the same way on the horizontal rows.

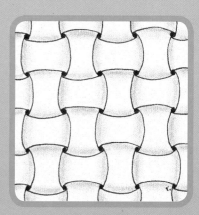

6. Add shading above and below every horizontal curve to finish.

Betweed

This tangle of overlapping layers works perfectly in triangular spaces.

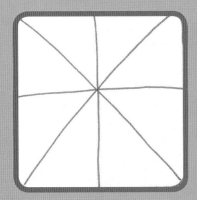

1. Start by drawing an "X" across the paper, and then draw a cross over it.

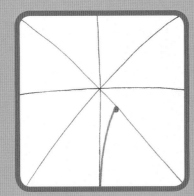

2. In one of the sections, draw a line from the bottom left corner that curves over to the right. When it touches the right line, add a small dot.

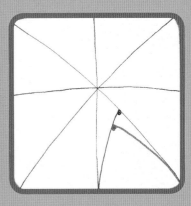

3. Now draw a line that curves from the bottom right corner and finishes further down the first curved line. Add a dot to the end of it.

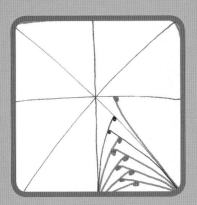

4. Repeat steps 2 and 3, adding curved lines and alternating from left to right until this section is full. Then move on to the next section, always starting in the left corner.

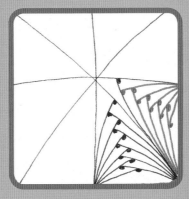

5. Repeat steps 2 to 4 until the second section is full.

6. Complete each section in the same way, always starting in the bottom left corner.

7. Add shading at the points where all the lines meet to complete the tangle.

Daviso

Bring a touch of magic to your fantasy pictures with this stunning star-spangled tangle!

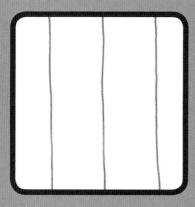

1. Draw evenly spaced vertical lines across the paper.

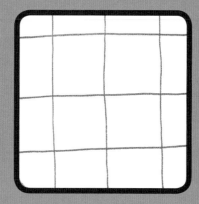

2. Add horizontal lines to form a grid.

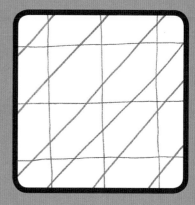

3. Now draw diagonal lines across the grid. Make sure that these lines do not cross the points where the horizontal and vertical lines meet.

4. Fill in all the triangles with your pen to make a pattern of stretched star shapes.

5. Your tangle is complete!

Tangle Tip!

Try to keep your diagonal lines as straight as possible, to make your tangle really pop!

Strings, Tangles, and ZIAs

The Zentangle® method begins with drawing "strings." These are pencil lines that separate spaces inside a shape. The spaces are then filled with tangles to create your ZIA. Each project in this book starts with an outline of a magical figure with the strings already drawn in.

These steps show you how to build up a set of Zentangle® patterns on a Zentangle® tile. Tiles are good for practicing the tangles you've just learned. They can also be works of art themselves!

1. To create a square tile, use a ruler and pencil to draw four evenly-spaced dots for the corners. Connect the dots with straight lines.

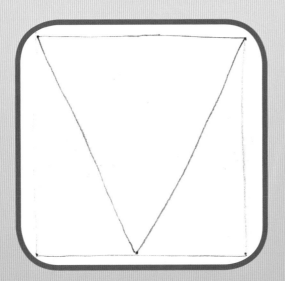

2. Now add strings to divide up the square. Draw a dot in the center of the bottom line. Then draw strings from the top corners to the new dot. This will create three triangle shapes to fill with tangles.

3. Choose a section to fill and a tangle to start with. We've chosen Printemps (page 9). Starting in one corner and using a pen, carefully fill the area with the tangle.

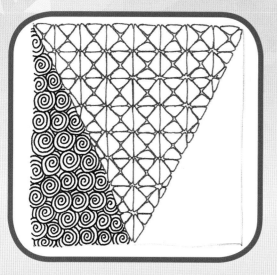

4. Now move to the next space created by the string. We've chosen to fill this section with 'Nzeppel (page 8).

5. In the final space, we've used Bales (page 7).

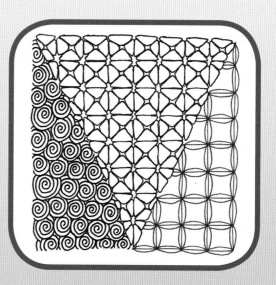

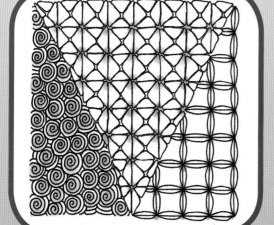

6. To complete the tangles, add shading to create shape and texture.

Now you're ready to start your own tangles!

Magical Unicorn

With tangles and imagination, you can create
a **prancing**, patterned unicorn.

1. Start by drawing
or tracing the outline
of your unicorn. Add
strings on its back for
your tangles.

2. We chose Vega as
the main tangle for
the unicorn, drawing
the lines at different
angles for the head,
neck, legs, and body.

3. We filled in the areas between the stripes in Vega for a really dramatic effect.

TANGLE KEY
Finery: page 13
Keeko: page 7
Printemps: page 9
Vega: page 10

4. We've used Finery for the unicorn's swishing mane and tail, Printemps for its swirly horn, and Keeko for its **hooves**.

21

Mystical Dragon

Dragons are often scary, scaly creatures that breathe fire. You can tangle a magnificent beast of your own with curly **spines**, spotty wings, and wonderful woven claws!

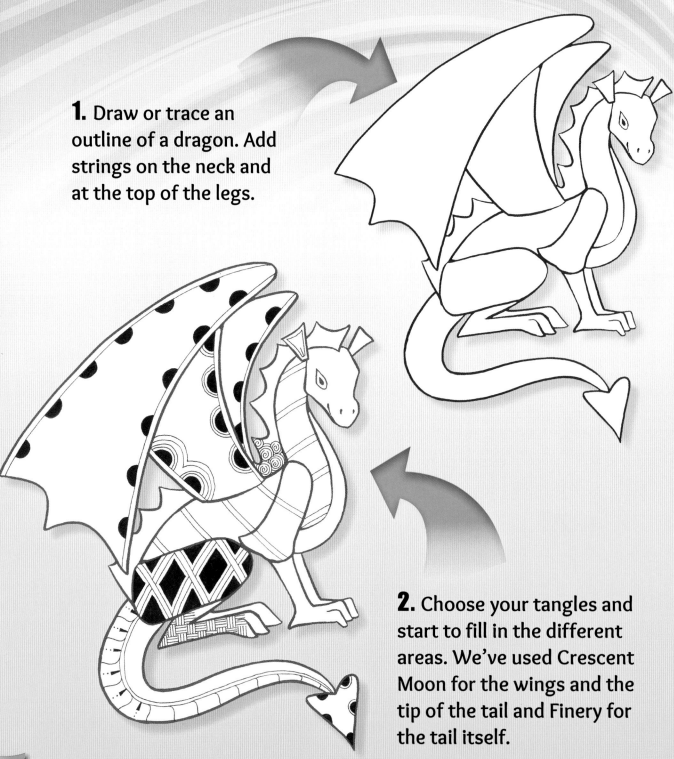

1. Draw or trace an outline of a dragon. Add strings on the neck and at the top of the legs.

2. Choose your tangles and start to fill in the different areas. We've used Crescent Moon for the wings and the tip of the tail and Finery for the tail itself.

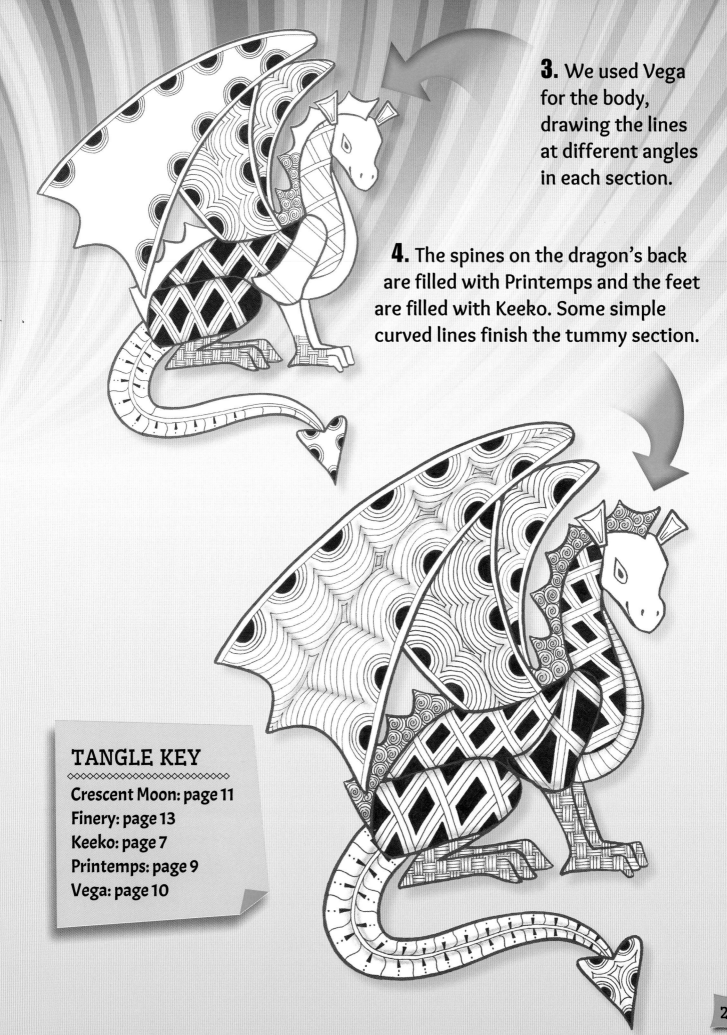

3. We used Vega for the body, drawing the lines at different angles in each section.

4. The spines on the dragon's back are filled with Printemps and the feet are filled with Keeko. Some simple curved lines finish the tummy section.

TANGLE KEY

Crescent Moon: page 11
Finery: page 13
Keeko: page 7
Printemps: page 9
Vega: page 10

Beautiful Phoenix

The phoenix is a mythical bird that lives for hundreds of years. Create your own Zentangle®-inspired version with wonderful outstretched wings and cleverly tangled tail feathers.

1. Draw a phoenix with four long tail feathers and two sections on each wing.

2. Begin to outline the tangles on the wings. We chose Jonqual for the main section and Tortuca for the inner wing.

3. We've filled the tail feathers with Betweed and the body with Finery to **contrast** with the bold pattern on the wings.

4. Add shading to the body, inner wings, and tail feathers to give your phoenix shape.

TANGLE KEY

Betweed: page 16
Finery: page 13
Jonqual: page 12
Tortuca: page 14

Ice Queen

Use tangles with sharp points and crisp edges to create
the perfect frosty gown for this beautiful ice queen
as she sweeps through her frozen palace.

1. Draw or trace an
ice queen with a spiky
crown and a layered gown.

2. Start to add tangles
to the outline. We used
'Nzeppel for the tips
of her icicle crown and
Betweed's overlapping
pattern for her collar.

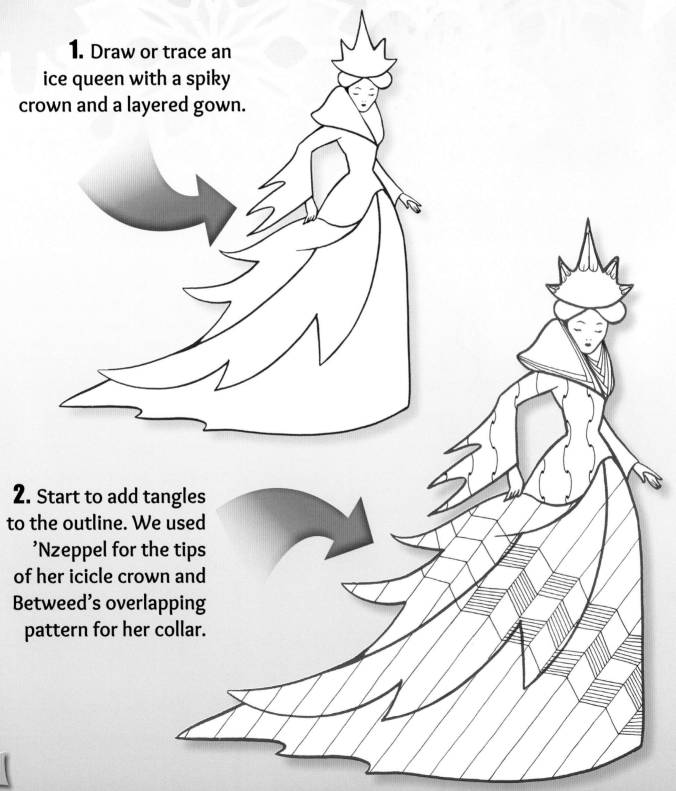

3. We chose Huggins for the top section of the gown and Jonqual for the skirt.

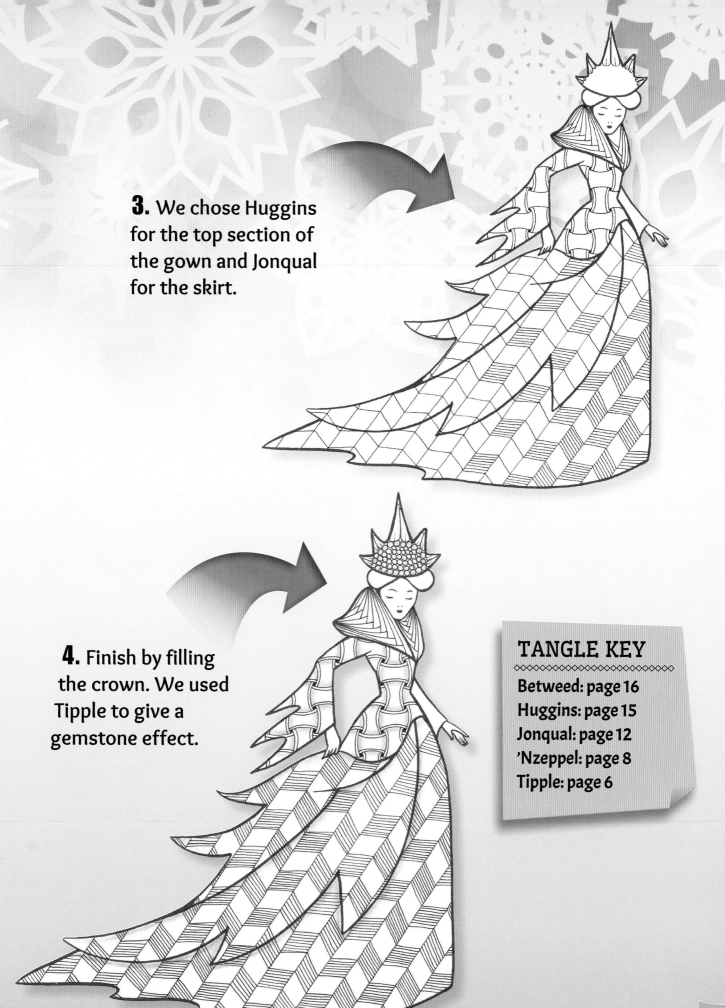

4. Finish by filling the crown. We used Tipple to give a gemstone effect.

TANGLE KEY

Betweed: page 16
Huggins: page 15
Jonqual: page 12
'Nzeppel: page 8
Tipple: page 6

Flower Fairy

Work your magic on this pretty fairy dressed in petals and fill your picture with flowery tangles.

1. Draw or trace a pretty fairy holding a flower. Add layers of petals to her dress to fill with lovely tangles.

2. Choose your tangles and begin to fill the sections. We've used Tipple for the middle of the flower and Daviso for the petals.

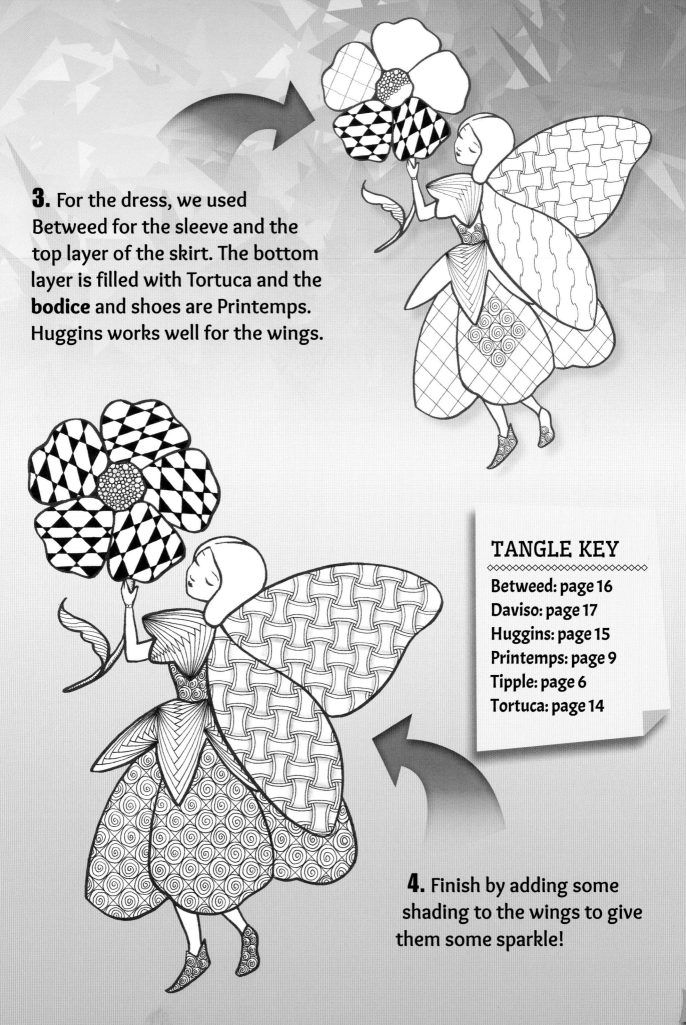

3. For the dress, we used Betweed for the sleeve and the top layer of the skirt. The bottom layer is filled with Tortuca and the **bodice** and shoes are Printemps. Huggins works well for the wings.

TANGLE KEY

Betweed: page 16
Daviso: page 17
Huggins: page 15
Printemps: page 9
Tipple: page 6
Tortuca: page 14

4. Finish by adding some shading to the wings to give them some sparkle!

Glossary

3-D Stands for "3 dimensional." If a drawing or pattern looks 3-D, it looks like a solid object.

bodice The middle section of a dress that covers the chest and stomach.

contrast To be strikingly different from something else.

diagonal A straight line at an angle.

grid A set of uniform squares made from straight lines or points

hooves The hard, bone-like part of the foot of some animals, including horses and cows.

horizontal A straight line that is parallel to the horizon, the imaginary line where the ground meets the sky.

mane Long hair growing on the neck of some animals, including horses.

mythical Coming from ancient stories known as myths.

pattern A set of shapes or a design that is repeated.

prancing Moving with dance-like steps.

spines Hard, spiky projections on the backs of some creatures.

spiral A shape made from a line moving outwards in a circular pattern from a central point.

texture The look or feel of a surface or substance.

vertical A straight line running from top to bottom, or bottom to top.

Further Information

Books to Read

Drawing Fantasy Monsters
Janos Jantner
PowerKids Press, 2013

Zentangle® for Kids
Jane Marbaix
Sterling Children's Books, 2015

Zentangle® for Kids: With Tangles, Templates, and Pages to Tangle On
Beate Winkler
Quarry Books, 2016

Websites

Find fairytale coloring pages at this magical site!
http://www.hellokids.com/r_1964/coloring-pages/fairy-tales-coloring-pages

Head over to this website for lots of Zentangle® coloring pages and other drawing tutorials.
http://www.supercoloring.com/coloring-pages/arts-culture/zentangle

Check out this website for Zentangle® coloring pages and lots of other activity ideas.
http://kidsactivitiesblog.com/?s=zentangle

Index